KU-581-304

Britain's Settlement by the Anglo-Saxons and Scots

Claire Throp

raintree

a Capstone company — publishers for children

Raintree is an imprint of Capstone Global Library Limited, a company incorporated in England and Wales having its registered office at 7 Pilgrim Street, London, EC4V 6LB – Registered company number: 6695582

www.raintree.co.uk
myorders@raintree.co.uk

Edited by Helen Cox-Cannons and Holly Beaumont
Designed by Richard Parker
Original illustrations © Capstone Global Library Limited 2015
Illustrated by Martin Sanders (Beehive Illustration)
Picture research by Svetlana Zhurkin and Pam Mitsakos
Production by Helen McCreath
Originated by Capstone Global Library Limited
Printed and bound in China by CTPS

ISBN 978 1 406 29108 7
18 17 16 15 14
10 9 8 7 6 5 4 3 2 1

British Library Cataloguing in Publication Data
A full catalogue record for this book is available from the British Library.

Acknowledgements
We would like to thank the following for permission to reproduce photographs: Alamy: Archimage, 14, Eyre, 17, Heritage Image Partnership Ltd, 27, qaphotos, 29; Bridgeman Images: Fitzwilliam Museum, University of Cambridge, UK, 25; Corbis: Homer Sykes, 24; Dreamstime: Colin Youn, cover inset (helmet); Getty Images: UIG, cover, UIG/Geography Photo, 15, UIG/Universal History Archive, 20; iStockphotos: duncan1890, 23; Newscom: akg-images/British Library, 19, WHA/United Archives/KPA, 18, World History Archive, 16, 26, ZUMA Press/Robin Nelson, 22; Shutterstock: Duncan Gilbert, 4, Hyena Reality, background (throughout), Karramba Production, cover (top left), back cover, Stanislav Petrov, background (throughout), Vadim Sadovski, 6—7 (back); SuperStock: age fotostock/Heinz-Dieter Falkenstein, 11, Nomad, 13.

We would like to thank Dr Mark Zumbuhl of the University of Oxford for his invaluable help in the preparation of this book.

Every effort has been made to contact copyright holders of material reproduced in this book. Any omissions will be rectified in subsequent printings if notice is given to the publisher.

Contents

Some words in this book appear in bold, **like this.** You can find out what they mean by looking in the glossary.

Goodbye to Rome

By AD 43, when the Romans **conquered** Britain, the Roman **Empire** was very powerful. The Romans brought their customs and inventions to Britain, including new foods and ideas about health and cleanliness. Many people in the south of Britain took up Roman ways. However, the Romans never managed to gain control of the north of Britain (what is now Scotland). They called the people who lived there Picts.

Hadrian's Wall was built from AD 122 to stop attacks from northern Britain.

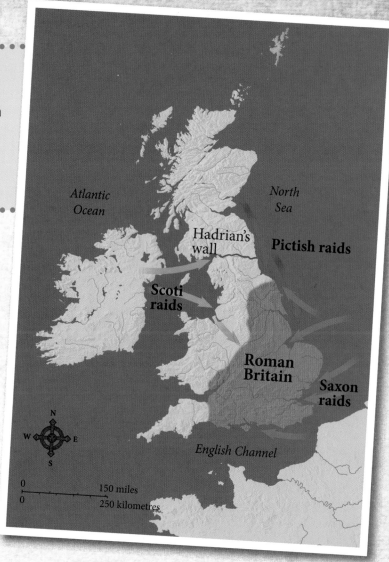

This map shows Britain in the early AD 400s.

Atlantic Ocean

North Sea

Hadrian's wall

Pictish raids

Scoti raids

Roman Britain

Saxon raids

N
W   E
S

0
0

150 miles
250 kilometres

English Channel

Attacks on Roman Britain

From the late AD 300s, the Romans began to leave Britain in order to defend other areas of their empire. But Britain needed defending too. From about AD 367, the Scoti (also known as the Scots) from Ireland had been attacking the north and west of England, while Picts attacked the north-east. Angles, Saxons and Jutes had been making **raids** in the south, too. The Britons had been used to the Roman army dealing with such attacks. They sent letters to Rome asking for help. They received some assistance in AD 397 or AD 398, but still the attacks continued.

By AD 407, the last two Roman legions had left Britain to fight in Gaul (now known as France). More attacks from the Picts and Scoti in 408 left the Britons desperate. A year later, they pushed out the remaining weak Roman officials from the cities and decided to fight for themselves.

TIMELINE

The Anglo-Saxon **invasion** and **settlement** of Britain happened over a number of years. This timeline will help you see what happened when.

> For an explanation of what AD and BC mean, please see the glossary on page 30.

AD 360s
England, then under Roman rule, is attacked by the Picts and Scoti (Scots)

AD 397
The Roman commander Stilicho helps Britain to defend against the Picts, Scoti and Saxons

AD 408
More attacks from the Picts, Scoti and Saxons

AD 409
Britons force out the remaining Roman officials

AD 410
The Romans leave Britain

AD 449
The British leader Vortigern hires Anglo-Saxons to help fight the Picts and Scoti

AD 563
Irish **monk** Columba sets up a **monastery** on Iona

c. 625
Burial (possibly of King Raedwald of East Anglia) made at Sutton Hoo

664
The Whitby Synod takes place to decide whether to use Ionan or Roman customs in England. It decides to use Roman customs for issues such as the date of Easter.

Early 700s
The Lindisfarne Gospels are created

731
Bede finishes writing the *Ecclesiastical History of the English People*

780s onwards
Offa's Dyke is built along the border with Wales

793
Vikings attack Lindisfarne

Invasion and settlement

Some people think that around AD 400, the north-west of Scotland was **raided** and settled by Scoti from north-eastern Ireland. They forced out the Picts or the Britons who had lived there before and set up the **kingdom** of Dál Riata.

WHAT'S THE LANGUAGE?

Scoti was a word used by the Romans to describe the people who raided Britain. It was also used to talk about people living in Ireland and in the west of what is now Scotland. These people became known as the Scots and the country of Scotland named after them.

ARCHAEOLOGISTS

One way we can find out what happened in Britain after the Romans left in the early AD 400s is to use archaeology. **Archaeologists** dig for objects from the past. They examine these objects to find out more about people or places from long ago.

However, other people think that the Scoti always lived in the west of Scotland, or at least had lived there for a very long time before AD 400. The western Scottish islands and the coast of Northern Ireland are only about 20 kilometres apart. The two countries fought and traded, so there were likely to be similarities in their **cultures**.

This map shows where the groups who **invaded** Britain in the AD 400s came from.

Anglo-Saxons

In the mid-AD 400s, Angles, Saxons and Jutes came to Britain from what are now northern Holland, northern Germany and Denmark. These invaders have come to be known as the Anglo-Saxons. There are different ideas about why they came to Britain. Some people think it was because Vortigern, a ruler in south-east England, needed help to defend against the attacks of Picts and Scoti in the north of England, and Saxon pirates in the south.

Another idea is that some Anglo-Saxons came looking for land to farm because their own lands often flooded. They may have thought that, with the Romans gone, it would be easy to attack Britain and claim land for themselves.

There were also some Anglo-Saxons in England before the **invasion**. The Roman Army used soldiers from all over the **empire**. Some came from the Germanic lands, and would have been working in Britain before the Romans left.

VORTIGERN

Vortigern lived in the AD 400s and was one of the top rulers in Britain. Not much is known about him. Some people think Vortigern is not a name but a title, meaning "high-king" or "over-ruler". Legends say that he came to be high-king by murdering his rivals.

Vortigern hired Prince Hengist and Prince Horsa from Jutland (north Holland) to help defeat the Picts and the Scoti.

Settlement

According to later written **texts**, some Anglo-Saxon rulers, such as Oisc Aelle of Sussex (the son of Hengist), and Cerdic of Wessex, fought battles against the Britons and **conquered** much of their land. We are not sure whether all these early Anglo-Saxon rulers really lived, but we do know that the Anglo-Saxon people took over a large part of England. The Anglo-Saxons gradually pushed the Britons westwards. Jutes settled in Kent, the Angles in East Anglia and Northumbria, and the Saxons in Essex, Sussex, Middlesex and Wessex.

This is how Britain looked in 550, after the Anglo-Saxon invasions.

At Dunadd in western Scotland, new Dál Riata kings would place one of their feet in the footprint in the rock as part of the crowning ceremony.

Sharing Britain

By the 600s, four groups shared Britain. Britons remained in Cornwall, Wales and Strathclyde (now the south-west of Scotland). Gaels (the Scoti) lived in Ireland, the Hebrides and west Scotland. Picts lived in eastern and north-eastern Scotland. The Anglo-Saxons had taken over the east and south of England. The most important Anglo-Saxon **kingdoms** by the 650s were Northumbria, East Anglia, Mercia, Wessex and Kent.

WHAT'S THE LANGUAGE?

The country came to be known as Angle-land after the Angles. This later became England.

Everyday life

The Anglo-Saxons had little interest in Roman roads, towns and buildings. However, it wasn't the case that everything Roman was destroyed straight away. They did live in some Roman towns, such as London, but mainly chose to live in villages or on farms.

The remains of an Anglo-Saxon village were discovered at West Stow in Suffolk. This home has been recreated using Anglo-Saxon ways of building.

WHAT'S THE LANGUAGE?

The Anglo-Saxon's language was called Englisc or Old English, which eventually became English. In Old English, *hus* means house and *land* means land! *Faeder* and *modor* mean father and mother.

Houses

Instead of moving into Roman stone houses, Anglo-Saxons built new homes. Houses had wattle and daub walls and thatched roofs. Wattle was made from small branches woven together and daub was a mixture of straw, mud and animal poo! The daub was plastered on top of the wattle to make the walls.

In many villages, a number of small houses were built around a large hall. Each house had a fire in the middle for heat and cooking. The house would have been smoky as there was no chimney. The whole family would live in the same house.

Place names

As the Anglo-Saxons pushed further west, villages were named after the most important man of the area. Worthing in East Sussex, for example, was known as Wurthingas – "Wurth's people". *Ham* meant homestead or **settlement**, so Birmingham was the homestead of Beorma's people.

The town of Saxmundham was named after a local man called Seismund.

Burials

When Anglo-Saxons died, they were often buried with their possessions, such as weapons, or dishes that held food or drink. These possessions are known as grave goods. The objects were meant to help the dead person in the **afterlife**. Men and women were often buried with different types of grave goods. Women were usually buried with jewellery and combs. Men had weapons and belt buckles. This type of burial stopped when the Anglo-Saxons **converted** to **Christianity**.

This silver bowl was one of the treasures found in the burial chamber at Sutton Hoo.

Sutton Hoo ship burial

Sutton Hoo in Suffolk is probably the best-known Anglo-Saxon burial place in Britain. When it was discovered in 1939, 41 gold objects were found inside a ship. There were also coins that allowed **archaeologists** to date the burial to about the year 625. The burial was probably for King Raedwald of East Anglia. He died in 624 or 625. The burial had both Christian and **pagan** features – King Raedwald had converted to Christianity but he later returned to being a pagan.

This display shows what the Sutton Hoo burial for King Raedwald would have looked like.

GRAVE GOODS

Much of what we know about the early Anglo-Saxons comes from grave goods. As well as the gold found at Sutton Hoo, there were also silver objects from Greece and a bowl from the Middle East. These objects show what kind of connections the East Anglian king Raedwald had around the world.

Culture

A **monk** called Bede wrote a book called the *Ecclesiastical History of the English People*. It is the first written history of England and helps us to understand what happened in the early Anglo-Saxon years. It is also the first book to use BC and AD in dates. Bede finished writing his book by 731.

BEDE

Bede was born around 673. At the age of seven, he went to St Peter's **monastery** in Wearmouth, Northumbria, to train to be a monk. When he finished his training, he moved to St Paul's monastery in Jarrow and lived there for the rest of his life. He wrote or translated about 40 books. Bede died in 735.

The Lindisfarne Gospels are thought to have been created by just one monk. This was possibly Eadfrith, who was Bishop of Lindisfarne from 698 to 721.

Art

One of the main types of Anglo-Saxon art is called manuscript illumination. Monks would copy the gospels of the Bible and draw pictures and patterns to decorate the pages.

The Lindisfarne Gospels were created in the early 700s at Lindisfarne Priory in Northumberland. The Gospels were handwritten, illustrated books that told the story of Jesus and his teachings.

Religion

Christianity had appeared in Britain during Roman times, and many Britons were Christians by the time the Anglo-Saxons arrived. The Anglo-Saxons brought their own religion.

Woden was the Anglo-Saxon version of Odin, a Scandinavian god. The Vikings from Scandinavia were pagan, too.

Anglo-Saxon gods

Early Anglo-Saxon religion was **pagan,** which meant they **worshipped** many gods.

The main Anglo-Saxon god was Woden. Thunor, Tiw and Frigg are other gods known to have been worshipped in Britain. Frigg was the goddess of motherhood, Tiw was the war god and Thunor was the thunder god.

Some of the names of days of the week we use today are based on Anglo-Saxon gods. For example, Wednesday is Woden's Day (*Wodnesdaeg*) and Friday is Frigg's Day.

Sometimes the gods' names were used for place names. These were areas where worship of that particular god took place. Thursley in Surrey and Thundersley in Essex are places where Thunor was worshipped. People in Wednesfield in Staffordshire worshipped Woden. Wednesfield means Woden's field.

THE DARK AGES

The AD 400s and 500s are sometimes called the Dark Ages. This is mainly because we have very little written information about these years.

The coming of Christianity

Many of the Gaels living in Dál Riata were already Christian when Columba, an Irish **monk**, arrived in northern Britain in 563. He and his 12 followers set up a **monastery** on Iona, a small island on the west coast of what is now Scotland. This monastery was important in helping to spread **Christianity**.

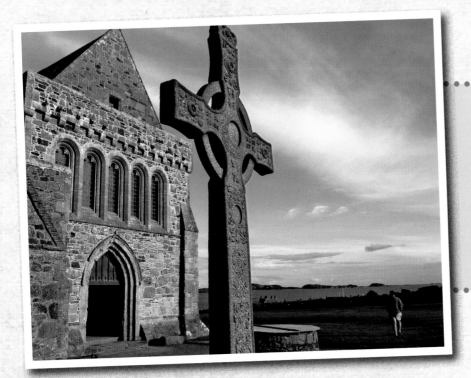

This Celtic cross is outside Iona Abbey. It represents Christianity.

CUTHBERT

Cuthbert was born in Northumbria in about 635. He was a soldier for a few years before going to the monastery at Melrose – now in the Borders in Scotland, but then part of Northumbria. He was made Bishop of Lindisfarne in 685 and died there in 687. He is best known for helping to spread Christianity in the north of England. His tomb became a place of miracles and **pilgrimage**.

The English

In 597, the Pope sent a bishop called Augustine to **convert** the English to Christianity. King Ethelbert of Kent, whose French wife was a Christian, gave St Martin's Church in Canterbury to Augustine. There, Augustine was allowed to teach Christianity. King Ethelbert was one of the first to convert.

Augustine was the first Archbishop of Canterbury.

The Whitby Synod

In 664, King Oswiu of Northumbria called for a meeting named the Whitby Synod. The meeting was to decide whether Northumbria should follow the customs of Rome or those from Ireland. These customs included the date of Easter and the way that monks wore their hair. Oswiu eventually decided that they would follow the Roman traditions.

War

During the early Anglo-Saxon years, **kingdoms** spent a lot of time fighting each other. A king did not always gain his crown by receiving it on the death of his father or other close relative. Sometimes he had to fight for it. This explains why kingdoms changed hands so often as one soldier defeated another and became the new king. Only successful warriors remained king for long.

Offa's Dyke, shown here, was built to stop Welsh warriors from attacking Offa's land in England.

OFFA

Mercia was the most powerful Anglo-Saxon kingdom in the 700s. Offa was king of Mercia from 757 to 796. He became king after his cousin King Aethelbald was murdered. From the 780s, Offa built a wall made of earth and a ditch (now known as Offa's Dyke) along the border between England and Wales.

A new type of silver penny was made during Offa's rule. The coins showed his name and title and were known as Offa's pennies.

The warrior code

In early Anglo-Saxon times, men were willing to fight and die for their leader. This was part of a strict warrior code. Most men were only part-time soldiers, though. They would fight for their ruler when needed, but most of the time they worked on their farms.

Armies and weapons

Anglo-Saxon armies usually had only several hundred men. Fighting normally took place on foot and face-to-face. Men carried weapons such as knives, axes, spears, swords and shields. Anglo-Saxon laws said that every man (apart from slaves) should own a spear. Men who owned swords were important, as swords were very expensive and difficult to make. Wealthier men wore helmets and chain mail armour to protect themselves while fighting. Poorer men wore leather waistcoats.

The Staffordshire Hoard contained more than 3,500 objects, including gold **foils** such as this one.

THE STAFFORDSHIRE HOARD

In 2009, objects and weapons from the mid-650s were found in a field near Lichfield in Staffordshire. The hoard was found near where a battle was fought between the Anglo-Saxons and the Welsh in Mercia in 655. Some people think the hoard was made up of the possessions taken from the losing side.

These spears and sword are old Anglo-Saxon weapons. The shield boss (the domed, middle part of the shield – shown here on the left) is the only part of the shield that remains. As it is made of iron, it would have protected the hand of the person holding the wooden shield.

Learning to fight

Boys were taught how to fight by the men of the **settlement.** The boys used wooden weapons at first. If a father owned a valuable sword, this would eventually be passed on to his son.

A new Britain

The Anglo-Saxons gradually took over most of England, pushing the Britons to Wales and Cornwall. By the late 700s, Mercia, Wessex and Northumbria were the most powerful **kingdoms**.

One of the big changes that the Anglo-Saxon invasion brought was the gradual destruction of Roman life in Britain. By about 600, many Roman buildings and roads had been allowed to crumble. Some towns, such as Exeter, were abandoned. Later, however, large Anglo-Saxon villages were built in what had once been Roman towns.

This map shows the main kingdoms of England around AD 700.

Atlantic Ocean

North Sea

NORTHUMBRIA

MERCIA

EAST ANGLIA

ESSEX

WESSEX

KENT

SUSSEX

English Channel

N
W   E
S

0   150 miles
0   250 kilometres

After the Anglo-Saxons **converted** to **Christianity,** they no longer used only wood for building. Early churches were made from wood, but later churches were built using stone.

There are very few written accounts of the early Anglo-Saxon years, so it is difficult to piece together exactly what happened during that time. Most of what we do know comes from archaeological finds. Grave goods and the remains of villages allow us to see how the early Anglo-Saxons lived.

Archaeologists **excavate settlements** in order to learn more about them.

Further invasions

From the late 700s, Britain faced yet more invasions. This time it was people from Denmark, Norway and Sweden — people known as the Vikings.

Glossary

AD dates after the birth of Christ; these count upwards so AD 20 is earlier than AD 25

afterlife place the Anglo-Saxons thought people went after death

archaeologist person who studies places and objects from the past

BC dates before the birth of Christ; these count downwards, so 25 BC is earlier than 20 BC

Christianity religion that teaches about the life of Jesus Christ

conquer take control of an area or country by force

convert to change religious beliefs

culture ideas, customs and behaviour of a particular group of people

empire countries under the rule of another country

excavate dig out material from under the ground

foil thin, bendable sheet of metal

invade try to take over a place or country by force

kingdom area ruled by a king

monastery place where monks live

monk very religious men who live in monasteries

pagan worship of many gods rather than just one

pilgrimage journey to a religious place such as a shrine

raid surprise attack

settlement place where people make their homes

texts book or other written information

worship take part in a religious ceremony

Find out more

Books

Life in Anglo-Saxon Britain (A Child's History of Britain),
Anita Ganeri (Raintree, 2014)

Men, Women and Children in Anglo-Saxon Times,
Jane Bingham (Wayland, 2011)

The Anglo-Saxons in Britain (Tracking Down),
Moira Butterfield (Franklin Watts, 2013)

Websites

www.bbc.co.uk/schools/primaryhistory/anglo_saxons
Discover everything you could want to know about the
Anglo-Saxons on this BBC website.

www.show.me.uk/topicpage/Anglo-Saxons.html
This website has information and activities on the
Anglo-Saxons from museums around the country.

Places to visit

If you want to visit some of the places in this book, such as
Sutton Hoo, find out more on the following websites:

The National Trust in England, Wales, and
Northern Ireland
www.nationaltrust.org.uk

The National Trust in Scotland
www.nts.org.uk

English Heritage
www.english-heritage.org.uk

Index